YOUR KNOWLEDGE HAS VALUE

- We will publish your bachelor's and master's thesis, essays and papers

- Your own eBook and book - sold worldwide in all relevant shops

- Earn money with each sale

Upload your text at www.GRIN.com and publish for free

Bibliographic information published by the German National Library:

The German National Library lists this publication in the National Bibliography; detailed bibliographic data are available on the Internet at http://dnb.dnb.de .

This book is copyright material and must not be copied, reproduced, transferred, distributed, leased, licensed or publicly performed or used in any way except as specifically permitted in writing by the publishers, as allowed under the terms and conditions under which it was purchased or as strictly permitted by applicable copyright law. Any unauthorized distribution or use of this text may be a direct infringement of the author s and publisher s rights and those responsible may be liable in law accordingly.

Imprint:

Copyright © 2018 GRIN Verlag
Print and binding: Books on Demand GmbH, Norderstedt Germany
ISBN: 9783668690714

This book at GRIN:

https://www.grin.com/document/420547

Seth Badu

Innovative Communication Technologies in Early Childhood Education and Related Issues

GRIN Verlag

GRIN - Your knowledge has value

Since its foundation in 1998, GRIN has specialized in publishing academic texts by students, college teachers and other academics as e-book and printed book. The website www.grin.com is an ideal platform for presenting term papers, final papers, scientific essays, dissertations and specialist books.

Visit us on the internet:

http://www.grin.com/

http://www.facebook.com/grincom

http://www.twitter.com/grin_com

Introduction

Contemporary issues are events, ideas, opinions or topics in a given subject area that are relevant to the present day (Arora, 2016). In the area of early childhood education, contemporary issues are issues that have come to light recently and are relevant to the present day.

ICT is becoming a ubiquitous component of the physical and social worlds occupied by young children. It is an important part of the private and work lives of most people, including those who support young children's learning and development, whether as parents, family members, caregivers, or early childhood educators. It is often argued in the literature that children's early childhood education experiences should reflect and connect with their experiences in the wider world. Therefore, ICT matters in early childhood education, because it already has an effect on the people and the environments that surround young children's learning and well-being. There is strong consensus across the literature that, it is timely for the role and potential of ICT for the early childhood education sector to be critically examined, to guide future development and decision-making in this area.

Since the inception of early childhood education program in 2004, there have several subjects of concern to ensure the effectiveness of the program and since the modern world is fast-paced and dynamic, these issues keeps coming into light and as early childhood stakeholders we cannot forgo these issues without discussing its relevance and effectiveness in advancing early childhood education in Ghana.

Why ICT is a contemporary issue in early childhood education

There is a growing recognition of the many different ways that ICT can contribute to or transform the activities, roles and relationships experienced by children and practitioners in early childhood settings. Much of available findings on ICT in early childhood education centers on the role and use of computers by young children. This is particularly true for most literature prior to 2006. However, in the few years there has also been a true growth in research and descriptive literature about the use of other kind of ICT in early childhood education including digital cameras, closed-circuit television, video conferencing, programmable toys, robotics and electronic musical instruments. There is also a growing focus of teachers using ICT with children, or on their own as a tool to support and scaffold children's early childhood education experiences to investigate and build learning experiences from children's interest or to strengthen relationships between children, practitioners and families.

Case studies and exemplars of the use of ICT in early childhood education settings are becoming more and more common. It is against this backdrop, I also wish to explore in the area ICT in early childhood education, its relevance, usefulness and effectiveness in advancing early childhood education in Ghana.

Relevance of ICT to early childhood education in Ghana

A look at researches in education over the years as well as several similar ICT frameworks in other countries indicate the emphasis being made on ICT in the early years. It can be seen from literature that a number of the studies express safety concerns with respect to integration of ICT in early childhood education and warn of several risks in this area. Some critics contend that technology in schools wastes time, money, and childhood itself by speeding up the pace and cutting down on essential learning experiences. An argument opposing early introduction of ICT is that, since children learn through their bodies, computers are not developmentally appropriate. This is because as a screen-based medium, activities at the computer are not as effective as manipulative in developing understanding and skills in the early years. He instead recommends that the developmental needs of young learners (whole-body movement, sensory interaction, focus on language, development of personal agency and the importance of relationships) take precedence in structuring effective early learning programs. In contrast to the above, current case studies and action research, such as the Children of the new millennium ICT research project, refute this view. It is widely accepted that appropriate use of ICT in early childhood settings, where there are skilled practitioners and quality ICT resources, has the potential to greatly enhance and support learning and development of young children. Some of the relevance of ICT to early childhood education in Ghana are discussed below:

1. The use of ICT provides a context for collaboration, co-operation, and positive learning experiences between children, or between children and adults. However, this will not necessarily happen of its own accord. Research indicates that practitioners must be conscious of the kinds of learning interactions they would like to occur in the context of ICT use (including between adults and children, or between children), and adopt pedagogical strategies to support these.

2. ICT provides a variety of ways for children to weave together words, pictures, and sounds, thereby providing a range of ways for children to communicate their ideas, thoughts, and feelings. Good software can allow children to engage in self-directed exploration, and can be tailored to children's individual needs, and assistive/adaptive ICTs can reduce barriers to participation for children with special physical or learning needs.

3. Case studies show how ICT can be used to support aspects of learning, including language development and the development of mathematical thinking.

4. ICT also provides unique opportunities for scaffolding and supporting learning for children with special learning needs, and children from culturally or linguistically diverse backgrounds.
5. ICT also presents opportunities for sharing and exchange of information between different services and agencies involved in children's care and education.
6. One of the most common uses of ICT in early childhood education settings relates to documentation of children's learning. Early childhood education centers with access to digital media build up electronic or physical portfolios of children's learning for assessment purposes, and to share with children and their families.
7. ICT strengthens and support family involvement in children's learning. Technology can inform and engagement of parents by enabling parents to receive and access information about their children's work, progress, attendance and behaviour when and where they want using , for example, secure online or even mobile access. ICT also enables parents to be more engaged with their child's learning which drives improvement.

How ICT can be made useful and effective in the advancement of early childhood education in Ghana.

In advancing information communication and technology in early childhood education in Ghana. The following ideas must be factored.

1. Curriculum policy must be put in place to bind the use of technological tools in the teaching and learning process in the classrooms as done in other countries like New Zealand. Emphasis therefore should be on the training of ICT teachers because they are the central forces for which the integration of ICT in children's learning will be made possible.

2. Government should increase the number of computers being given to the various schools as well as provide to the schools other technological resources like the cameras, closed-circuit television sets, programmable toys, projectors, tape recorders and electronic whiteboards etc. to enhance teaching and learning. .

3. There should be a continuous professional development through in-service training such as workshops and special short courses. The role of ICT with young children is a changing one, as new technologies developed will require different skills and aptitudes, and different challenges for pedagogy and practice. Alongside the ever-changing nature of ICT within the early years setting and the advancing technologies that staff will need to familiarize themselves with, the turnover of early year's staff will also need to be considered. In order to sustain and support the processes of identifying and evaluating these changes, professional development will need to continually evolve. It will be necessary to ensure that delivery models are designed to reflect staff needs and, in turn, effectively support children's learning.

4. Early childhood educators need to engage in a reflective process if they are to use ICT to its greatest potential. They need to ask themselves about the value of the ICT resources that they are using. Software resources also can be subjected to similar questions, if ICT is to be used effectively to promote children's learning and development. Software evaluation services can help but early year's educators need to be aware of the implicit assumptions

about children's learning that inform development of software packages. In further developing effective pedagogy, early childhood educators should:

- Develop practice for helping children to learn as they use an ICT resource alone or with others.
- Value and act on children's choices.
- Think critically about their own role in promoting individual children's learning.
- Develop procedures for planning, observing and recording children's use of ICT.
- Select resources in accordance with knowledge of children's development.
- Participate in the ongoing debate about the usefulness of ICT for young children.
- Be more aware of the wide variety of ICT resources that are available.
- Recognize, value and use children's experience of ICT outside the early years setting as an important learning resource.
- Take up the new opportunities that ICT can offer to become involved in partnership with parents and with local and wider communities.
- Support and value cultural identities and diversity by an appropriate use of the internet
- Provide more information and support about the range of resources that can be particularly effective in promoting inclusive practice
- Provide information and support about the use of ICT to support children's individual learning styles
- Maximize the potential for using ICT to support continuity in children's learning.

Conclusion

The term "ICT" encompasses much more than just computers. ICT can be defined as "anything which allows us to get information, to communicate with each other, or to have an effect on the environment using electronic or digital equipment".

The literature suggests at least three reasons why ICT matters in early childhood education. Firstly, ICT already has an effect on the people and environments that surround young children's learning. Secondly, these technologies offer new opportunities to strengthen many aspects of early childhood education practice. Thirdly, there is support and interest across the whole education sector for the development and integration of ICT into education policy, curriculum, and practice. There is a growing recognition of the many different ways in which ICT can contribute to, or transform the activities, roles, and relationships experienced by children and adults in early childhood education settings.

Many authors argue that because ICT will be a significant part of children's current and future learning environments, it is important for them to begin to develop ICT capability and "ICT literacy", and that early childhood education experiences have a role to play in this respect.

Reference

Becta, (2008). Exploiting ICT to improve parental engagement, moving towards online reporting, Millburn Hill Road.

Becta (2002). The impact of information and communication technologies on pupils learning and attainment.

Bolstad R. (2004). The role and potential of ICT in Early Childhood Education. A review of New Zealand and international literature. New Zealand council for educational research, Wellington.

Nsiah Asante J. (2014). The state of ICT integration in the early years in Ghana schools.

YOUR KNOWLEDGE HAS VALUE

- We will publish your bachelor's and master's thesis, essays and papers

- Your own eBook and book - sold worldwide in all relevant shops

- Earn money with each sale

Upload your text at www.GRIN.com
and publish for free